CW00859819

Early Reader Rhyming Riddles
Exotic Animals

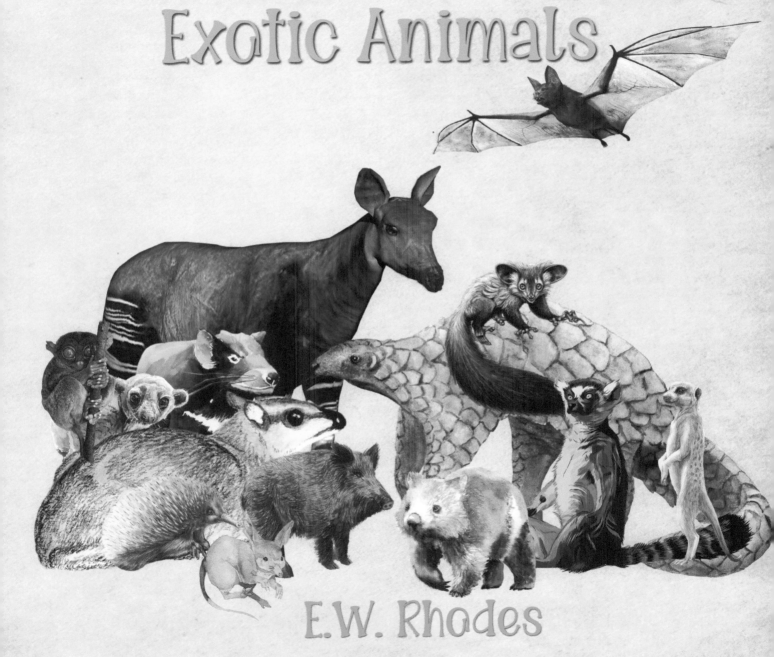

E.W. Rhodes

© Timeless Tales Press, 2021

First published in 2021

Written by E.W. Rhodes
Creative Consultant - S.B. Christian
Interior page design Bryony van der Merwe

ISBN: 978-1-954983-36-6 (paperback)
ISBN: 978-1-954983-37-3 (hardcover)
ISBN: 978-1-954983-35-9 (electronic)

Published by:

Timeless Tales Press, admin@timelesstalespress.com/timelesstalespress.com

This is for

**Mimi, Cee Cee,
Keegan, Sadie, Holden**

and all of those who are entering
the magical world
of reading.

Few people know me.
Some say that I'm odd.
I'll give you some clues.
Please give me a nod.

My fingers are long.
My teeth grow and grow.

I don't sleep at night.
Don't you know? Don't you know?

Please guess who I am,
before I say good-bye.

I'm on the next page.
I am an ...

Aye-aye

Few people know me.
Some say that I'm odd.
I'll give you some clues.
Please give me a nod.

I have a pouch on my back.
My tail is stubby.

My legs are short.
I look rather chubby.

Do you know who I am?
I am not a rat.

I'm on the next page.
I am a ...

Wombat

Few people know me.
Some say that I'm odd.

I'll give you some clues.
Please give me a nod.

My teeth are quite sharp.
My eyesight is keen.

I sleep all day long.
So, I'm rarely seen.

Do you know who I am?
If you do then you do.

I'm on the next page.
I am a ...

Kinkajou

Few people know me.
Some say that I'm odd.
I'll give you some clues.
Please give me a nod.

I am the only mammal with
scales on my back.

I don't sleep at night.
I eat termites for a snack.

Do you know me?
Don't leave me a-danglin'.

I'm on the next page.
I am a ...

pangolin

Few people know me.
Some say that I'm odd.

I'll give you some clues.
Please give me a nod.

My body is small.
I have very large eyes.

I love to eat insects.

Oh my, oh my.

Guess who I am.
You don't have to be sure.

I'm on the next page.
I am a ...

Tarsier

Few people know me.
Some say that I'm odd.
I'll give you some clues.
Please give me a nod.

My tail is short.
My wings are long.

I hunt for my prey
all night long.

I hope you know me.
I'd love to hear that!

I'm on the next page.
I am a ...

Vampire bat

Few people know me.
Some say that I'm odd.
I'll give you some clues.
Please give me a nod.

I have five fingers and toes and
can leap rather high.

I have a fairly long snout.
Oh my, oh my.

If you don't know me,
don't be a dreamer.

I'm on the next page.
I am a ...

Lemur

Few people know me.
Some say that I'm odd.

I'll give you some clues.
Please give me a nod.

I eat grasses from fields.

I eat bark from some trees.

I have a barrel-like body and a
short head don't you see.

Guess who I am.
Yes, guess, I dare ya'.

I'm on the next page.

I am a ...

Capybara

Few people know me.
Some say that I'm odd.
I'll give you some clues.
Please give me a nod.

I am medium sized with
thick hair and spines.

I have a tongue in my snout.
I look rather fine.

Do you know who I am?
Am I an enigma?

I'm on the next page.
I am an ...

Echidna

Few people know me.
Some say that I'm odd.

I'll give you some clues.
Please give me a nod.

My tail, it is tapered.
My legs are quite long.

My snout is pointed.

This isn't a song.

If you think you know me,
please tip your hat.

I'm on the next page.
I am a ...

Meerkat

Few people know me.
Some say that I'm odd.
I'll give you some clues.
Please give me a nod.

I'm small like a mouse.
I look like a deer.

My teeth are quite long.
Do you think that I'm weird?

Do you know who I am?
Do you think I look plain?

I'm on the next page.
I am a ...

Chevrotain

Few people know me.
Some say that I'm odd.
I'll give you some clues.
Please give me a nod.

I have a squat build with a
rather large head.

I hunt through the night.
My clues are all said.

Do you know who I am.
Please keep it on the level.

I'm on the next page.
I am a ...

Tasmanian
devil

Few people know me.
Some say that I'm odd.
I'll give you some clues.
Please give me a nod.

I have rabbit-like ears.
I have a tail that is long.

My body is small.
I can't sing a song.

If you do not know me,
I won't think you're silly.

I'm on the next page.
I am a ...

Bilby

Few people know me.
Some say that I'm odd.
I'll give you some clues.
Please give me a nod.

I have stripes on my legs.
My ankles are white.

Giraffes are my cousins.
Yes, you heard me right.

I groom myself with my tongue.
I never look sloppy.

I'm on the next page.
I am a ...

Okapi

Early Reader Rhyming Riddle Series

Timeless Tales Press's Rhyming Riddler Series is rooted in three objectives. First, our Early Readers aim to engage youngsters' reading fundamentally based on repetitiveness and rhyme. Second, the Rhyming Riddler Series provides children with basic knowledge of the world around them. And finally, successfully solving any of the riddles in each volume bolsters confidence, the appetite for learning, and the desire to read.

Please play with us in our Rhyming Riddler Series.

www.timelesstalespress.com

Other books by Timeless Tales Press

www.timelesstalespress.com

Lightning Source UK Ltd.
Milton Keynes UK
UKHW050415010921
389818UK00002B/16